What happens when
Wheels
Turn?

Daphne Butler

SIMON & SCHUSTER
YOUNG BOOKS

This book was conceived for
Simon & Schuster Young Books by
Globe Enterprises of Nantwich, Cheshire

Design: SPL Design
Photographs: Zefa except for
The Image Bank (7t, 8tr, 12l, 13, 14, 16, 22, 23, 26, 29)

First published in Great Britain in 1993
by Simon & Schuster Young Books
Campus 400, Maylands Avenue
Hemel Hempstead, Herts HP2 7EZ

© 1993 Globe Enterprises

Printed and bound in Singapore
by Kim Hup Lee Printing Co Pte Ltd

A catalogue record for this book is available
from the British Library
ISBN 0 7500 1284 6

Contents

A new technology

More than 5,000 years ago, people discovered a new technology that changed their lives.

The idea was probably sparked off by using the trunks of small trees as rollers.

Before long, people invented carts with wheels that could carry their goods and belongings wherever they wanted.

Changing wheels

Over the years, people improved the technology.

They gave wheels spokes to make them lighter and added iron rims to make them stronger.

Today, wheels have strong metal hubs and thick rubber tyres filled with air. They can travel at great speed.

More wheels

Wheels are used in many ways.

They are used in water as paddles to drive boats along and in air as rotor blades to lift helicopters.

They are also used in other vehicles. Can you name any?

Not just transport

Wheels provide a lot of fun!

What other wheels can you think of that give you a good time?

Can wheels be dangerous?

13

14

A swiftly spinning wheel with sharp
teeth cuts quickly through planks
of wood. It's called a circular saw
and it makes a horrible noise.

The teeth are kept very sharp by
using a special tool.

Grinding wheels

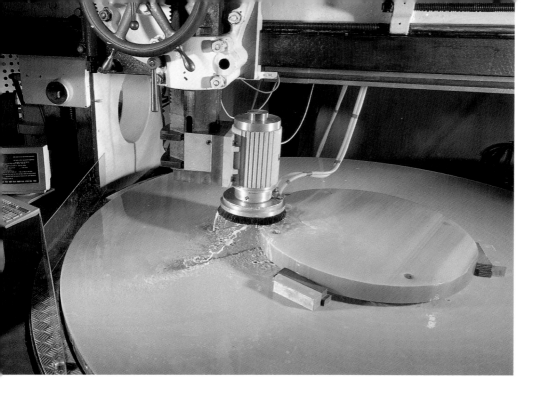

Grinding wheels are made of hard stone. They spin round quickly.

Objects touching them are worn silky smooth. Sometimes liquid is used to wash away the grindings.

Paper

Freshly made paper is wound onto rollers.

Toilet paper is wound onto small cardboard rollers so you can pull it off a sheet at a time.

Newspaper is wound onto huge cylinders that fit printing machines. When the wheels turn, folded newspapers appear at the other end of the machine.

This machine is weaving red cloth.
At the back you can see where
the threads come from.

Without wheels, reels and rollers
it could not work at all.

Cog wheels

Inside an old-fashioned watch or clock, there are many wheels with teeth round the edge. The teeth fit together so when one wheel turns, they all turn—these are cog wheels.

When cog wheels are of different sizes, the smaller ones must move faster to keep up with the bigger ones. Can you see why?

Cog wheels are an important part of most machines.

23

This machine uses cog wheels to help pump water out of a well.

The animal turns the horizontal cog wheel as it walks round and round. This turns the vertical wheel which joins to the wheel fitted with the jars.

The jars lift water out of the well and tip it into the gulley at the top.

Powerful wheels

Water wheels called turbines make electricity. When water or steam rushes past the turbine blades, they spin round turning a motor that makes the electricity.

turbine blades

What would your life be like
without wheels or electricity?

Wheel words

axle A fixed bar that joins two wheels together but allows them to turn.

conveyor belt
A band running on rollers that moves things from one place to another.

cogs A wheel with teeth round the outside.

gears A set of cog wheels which connect an engine to the wheels of its vehicle.

28

hub The central part of a wheel where the axle fits.

pulley A wheel with a groove round the edge in which a rope or cord fits. Pulleys allow heavy loads to be lifted more easily.

puncture A hole particularly in a rubber tyre.

tyre A rubber cushion that fits round a wheel and is usually filled with air.

29

Index